Signpost For the Lost
and Found

(And other selected poems)

I dedicate this book to Jesus Christ, my saviour, for his continual faithfulness, mercy and inspiration. No man 'spake like him', nor lived like him. Thirty three years, in the hands of such a master, shaped not only history but eternity. And as the scriptures say, all things were made through him and for him. And in him, we live, and move, and have our being.

And he lives now, and forever and lives ever to make intercession for us.

With grateful thanks and praise,

M. Joseph Burt

17/08/2023

Contents

"And even though it all went wrong
I'll stand before the Lord of Song
With nothing on my tongue but
Hallelujah"

~Leonard Cohen, Hallelujah~

1. Love Sits with You in The Ashes

There is no fear,
In love,

Love is not accolade,
It is not high praise,
From people,
Who don't really know you,
Love is not infatuation,
The fizzing disprin,
In your glass of stale water,
To make a brief disturbance in the calm,
And take the edge off the pain,
Then to wear off,

Love is not the loyalty,
Of friends nor lovers,
Who stand by your side
So long as it is mutually convenient,
Before there are sides to take,
Love sits with you,
In the ashes of your burned down life,

And Love lays with you,
The very first brick
On the foundation of truth,
And the second,
And the third...

And finally, when all the building is complete,
Love is the capstone,
Love wipes its brow,
(While you look on),
And says,
"There, It is finished,
Look what we have done!"

There is no fear in love,

Love knows us,
And never rejects us,

If love ever left you,
It was not Love,
If love ever turned its back on you,
It was not Love,
If love became over familiar,
It was not Love,

Because Love never fails,
Because Love remains.

Love is often imitated,
It inspires many,
But few can pull it off,
Because love stands with you on the heights,
Love looks for you in the depths,
Love hears when your heart cries in silence,
Love sees when you are all alone,

Love never fails.

2. This Should Not Be

My brothers, this should not be,
That with the same mouth,
I bless my maker,
And curse what he has made,

My familiar, this should not be,
That with the freedom,
Won with his forgiveness,
I should hold you a prisoner to my bitterness,

My Tribe, this should not be,
That we who were included when we were far off,
Should shun the ones who don't fit the mould,
Or seek exclusivity's fold,

My dear ones, this should not be,
That we who follow the one who would not cast a
stone,
Follow him around with armfuls of rocks,
To silence his "enemies",
My people this should not be.

My brothers, this should not be,
That we who are enslaved to our religion,
Should catch planes over the sea,
To win a single convert to our hypocrisy.

Can salt and fresh water flow from the same stream?
Sisters and brothers, this should not be.

3. Well Done Son

At the end of all days,
To hear the words
Well done son,
Like over-cooked toast,
Rescued from the flames.

4. Thank You for The Cost

(to the tune of Graham Kendricks "Thank you for the cross")

Thank you for the cost,
The price you loaned to us,
Where you gave yourself,
In lieu of interest,

Precious Lord, (Precious Lord),

Calvary's work is done,
All forgiven,
So we can pay you back,
When the day of judgement comes,

Thank you Lord, (thanks a lot),

Oh I'm saving Lord,
Really saving Lord,
Enough good works for me to hope to pay the fee,
You're my banker now,
You're the one I owe,
And the scariest thing of all oh Lord I see,
Is what you expect from me.

5. The Passengers

We are just passengers,
In this car called history,

We can act up,
Wriggle about,
On the back seat,
Make a bit of noise,
Sing a song or two,
But we will not change,
Its' destination,

One,
Little,
Bit.

6. Flood

The floods came,
They came, they came,
They took everything,
Everything,
Took it in their game,

The sky came,
And opened its heart to me,
And poured its hard tears down,

As the waters rose,
They rose, they rose,
Like a fast approaching date,
Like the devil in my destiny,
Like the unsealing of a fate,
The waters rose to float my resolve,
Clean out through the flood gate,
And heavens' gate can wait,

And heavens' gate can wait,
Can wait,
Till the tide of love's receded,
The flotsam of this fickle heart,
The jetsam of victories conceded,
Leaves debris on my banks,
Like dissent amongst the ranks.

For what the flood took,
And what the flood brought,
Have filled my fragile landscape,
And bought my resolve,
To nought.

The muds came,
They came, they came,
The softened earth sucks in,
Every foot that would walk in it,
Like love has softened sin,

Come walk a mile or two with me now,
Walk a mile beside the river,
You'll find the terrain quite different now,
The catastrophic event,
Has proved a real forgiver.

7. The Emptiness

An empty place in heaven,
The Son has left for a while,
The absence of his laughter,
Is everywhere.

An empty space in a manger,
The child has grown into a man,
The place of his arrival,
Is but a stepping stone.

An empty place on the cross,
The saviour has come to nothing,
The jeering winds of mocking tongues,
Still whistle past its' wood.

An empty ache in disciples hearts,
Their world has fallen apart,
They've been woken with a start,
From the sleeping where they dreamt of thrones.

An empty place within a tomb,
He is risen from the dead,
An empty claim death had on him,
He's back just like he said.

An empty sky where they stand,
And stare...

8. Poem For No-one

This is a nothing poem,
A nobody verse,
There's no-one known,
There's nothing worse,
No sigh more alone,
Than a corpse in a hearse,
Than an unanswered phone,
In the home of the cursed,
An echoing drone,
In search of reverse,

The poem of a dead man,
The knowing of his dead-pan plan.
Like the sonar of a bat like man,
Feeling his way,
Through the echo of the ricochet.

HELLO, hello, hello,
Is there anybody out there?
Just scream,
If,
You,
Can,
Hear,
Me.

The poem of a dead poet
Who's a dead man,
But,
Doesn't,
Yet,
Know it.

9. The Wisdom of Goldfish

We are Such very clever goldfish,
We know almost all the bowl,
From one glass side to the other,
Partial knowledge fills the whole.

We can even see out beyond the glass,
To blurred images of the gods,
That send down precious flakes from heaven,
That falls most every morning,
No matter what the odds,

We speculate about what we see and where they go,
When they go out through the door:
The outer reaches of the universe,
Our top scientists are pretty sure.

We are such clever fish,
We've come to this conclusion,
That the first fish in the bowl arrived here from a piece
of algae,
By the process of evolution.

We can rest assured now,
That we know most everything,
And if there's a flaw in our logic,
Well, ignorance is king.

10.   Notification

Looking all day for the little red box,
Scanning my phone to find out what's what,
A reply, a like, a post from a "close friend",
My mind on my Facebook,
When does it end?
Notify me,
I have to see.

Real life events (on a real timeline) are passing me by,
My wife up and left me and I never asked why,
I commented on her relationship status,
"It's complicated" actually means that she hates us.
Notify me,
I can hardly see.

All day long the ancient of days,
Holds out his hands, shows us his face,
But the notification doesn't come on my phone,
So, sadly, I miss the alert when it's shown,
God, notify me.
I need to see.

The vibration setting of a tuned in spirit,
The alert of nature can cause you to hear it,
The love of real friends can give you a taste,
Of the eternal love in the book of the face, of the king,
Incoming,
"He loves you,
You're wanted",
Ping.

Notification, every minute, every day,
Father cares is what The Son says.
This is the notification,
Of your salvation.
O Lord,
Notify me,
I want to see.

"Jesus Christ, the same:
Yesterday, today and
forever."

~Hebrews 13:8~

11.   Apathetic Accounting

If the wages of sin are death,
And the godless are godless still
As they spend their dying breath,
Their earthly credit has expired,
Now they give their account,
Draw on their damned pension, once retired,
Who are we saving from the fires?

Do we sit on our nest egg
Whilst they are forced to beg?

When weighing up the cost,
Of reaching out to the lost,
Do we charge it to you or I?

Let's split the indifference.

12.   Home

A home,
A nest,
A place near you altar,
A lasting rest,

I lay this sleeping-bag-body down,
I lay my home,
Where ever your heart is,

It's were the start was,
It's where the end is,
That's my home.

It has a door,
That's open to strangers.
Closed to the dangers,
A welcome, cosy fortress,
My mattress,
Is in you.

When I sleep,
When I wake,
I am with you.

When I sleep,
If I make,
My bed on the far side of the sea,
When I wake,
You're with me.

My home,
My home,
My home.

(Psalm 84 & Psalm 139)

13.   One Last Flourish

A final year like Keats',
Poem-strewn floor,
Like flowers at my feet,
As the wedding arrives,
After 52 weeks,
And lasts but a day in the sun,
And, for a few more years, the marriage continues to
run,
Or limp on,
A blossoming climax in the summer sun,

After a lifetime of being buried,
The seeds journey is done,
The cycle complete,
The circle's become,
Full,
And fat,
And rotund,
And now that it's gone
Now that I've drained the fund,
The suffering is worth what has become,
A life spent in dirt,
For my moment of Sun,

To stretch out the petals and unfurl,
To silence the voices,
To show the girl,
What she's lost,

For a moment like that,
It's worth all the cost,

One aggressive, defiant last charge at lifes' gate,
One Light-brigade shout,
One Samson style take,
The pillars out that support their mistake,
To think that they've got you down,

Burn out and shine in the heat,
Or slowly drown.

For one last year like Keats,
Poem-strewn life,
Like flowers at my feet.

14.   Tree-Hugger

The solution sprang from the soil,
The soul of the soil,
The life of the earth,
At first trees muddy birth,
As sinews snaked from seed,
And belly crawled towards the light,
For more of the warmth that hugged the brown earth,
That stirred it so,
That raised its' sap,
To start with.

The light welcomed its' emergence with enthusiasm,
Caressed its' budding leaves with its' soft yellow rays,
The tree had knowledge,
The tree knew the garden,
For the first time,
Before the gardener began,
And it was good.
Before man,

It was abuse of the tree,
The wrongful use,
Of right, ripe fruit,
That gave way,
To the gateway,
For great decay,
The garden gives up its guardians,
As rotten to the core,

The trees sway a farewell,
As they gaze on the heel of Adam,
As it disappears on the horizon.

And the solution came from the soil
The healing was in the tree,
The tree cleansed the very air,
That gave wind to man's lies,
The tree lent its support,
To the wait of the saviour,
Bore him,
For just a little longer,

As Christ clung,
The Trees' embrace lifted him,
Crimson and Glorified,
Like the hand of a mid-wife presents the baby,
To the waiting world.

The solution sprung from the soil,
As the sap, sent down, revived it,
The sap of the righteous tree,
Whose oaky sap was shed for me,

That all men shall be saved,
When they embrace the tree.

15. Justified

I concede,
We all need,
To feel we are Justified,
It's just, I lied

I'm just the same,
Just as bad,
Just as lame,
But just as glad I came,

Leaping out from,
Just beyond the frame
Just as if,
I made this game,
I just wanted you,
To know my name,

So, I'm Justified,
And not to blame.

16.   Judah

Look at me,
Walking along,
With a king size Poop-a-scoop,
And a Lion on a lead.

I think I have him under control,
I've been training him for many years,
Rewarding him with bits of meat,
And tickling his ears.

He even does the odd trick for me,
(Though he won't perform for strangers),
They think us a little bit insane,
And, if I'm honest, rather dangerous,

So, I put bunches in his mane,
And pink ribbons on his tail,
To make him more acceptable,
(And to keep me out of jail!)

I sometimes want to introduce him,
To the people that I meet,
But for some unfathomable reason,
They just run off down the street.

Sometimes when I have new company,
I keep him in the room next door,
And make up my excuses,
If they hear him roar,

I love my Lion very much,
But I have my pride,
What would the new neighbours think,
Knowing I have a lion inside?

On the odd occasion,
When we're out and about,
I wonder if the lead I've got him on,
Is really all that stout,

But I am pretty sure,
That it's me that's in control,
Of this Lion called Judah,
On our gentle stroll.

17.   Simple Faith

I want to be clever,
To work this out,
To arrive at the answer,
To eradicate doubt,

I want to get it right,
To tick all the boxes,
But my tick wont fit,
And that's what the shock is.

The 't' won't be crossed,
The 'i' won't stay dotted,
The ink like blood has spilt,
My mental page is blotted.

I can't unsee what,
I've seen from a boy,
I can't ignore the feelings,
I chose to employ,

The twin hounds of faith,
And doubt, have grabbed one leg each,
They're tearing my trousers,
With razor sharp teeth,

And as they pull,
And fight for my jeans,
It seems what's neglected,
Is the Man underneath.
And I come to realise,
That it's not faith but beliefs,
That I can shed these trousers,
And walk off in my briefs,
Hand in hand with my saviour,

This simple act of faith,
Is a complex act of trust,
A resigning of self,
But an all-essential must.

18.   Ministry

Your ministry is not chemistry,
Nor alchemy or sorcery,
It is not fakery nor forgery,
Not trickery nor mimicry,

It's not intelligence,
Nor is it your 50 cents,
Not your pound of flesh,
Not indulgence for your interests.

Not a means of gaining praise,
Not a passing phase, to fill some days,
It is not for you to fill your pockets as you tread the
grain,
It's not for you, I will say it again,

It is not,
For you.

Your ministry,
Is service.
All the rest,
Is worthless.

19.   I am Grateful

For the times when time is still as a rock
For the times when I stop clocking the watch,
Or watching the clock,
For the times when I am the boat,
And time is the dock,
For the stillness,
I am grateful,

For the relief that comes after pain,
And for the pain,
They're one and the same,
Two roads converging to run as one lane,
And for the Journey,
I am grateful,

For loyalties and abuses of trust,
Betrayals and friendships are just,
A refining of gold from dust,
The sifting process does what it must,
For the lessons in true value,
I am grateful,

For all the saints that have gone before,
For all the teachers who held open the door,
For those who have scraped my remains from the floor,
I'd be nothing without you, I am utterly sure,
For the comfort of unaware Angels,
I thank you.

For the divine and loving thread
From before conception, till long after I'm dead,
To that bridegroom eternally wed,
When mountains have sunk let it be said

We bled,
Together.

For you,
I'm eternally grateful.

20.   Turn The Page

Whatever you did 5 minutes ago,
That so filled your heart with shame and rage,
Beneath the blood it is forgotten,
That was another age,
Forgive yourself and,

Turn the page.

Every day was written in,
Before one of them came to be your cage,
But in the book of life and grace,
The script's as blank as an empty stage,
Learn your lines and improvise,
Play your part and,

Turn the page.

Whatever the grave clothes you wear,
From your former deathly wage,
The plot line demands that you take them off,
Be you sinner, saint or sage,
Shed regret and pain and naked to new life,
Come forth and take the stage,
The old you has been written out, so,

Turn the page.

"I am the way, the truth and the life. No one comes to the Father but by me"

~John 14:6~

21.   Signpost
(for The Lost and Found)

And there it was
For all to see
The glory of
Your majesty,
The cross of wood
There in the ground
The signpost for
The lost and found,

Lifted high
For all to see
Your power
 And humility,
We look on you
In all your pain,
To live is Christ,
To die is gain,

Lifted up
For a little while,
The bearer of
All that's vile,
We look upon
Our sin and live
Humbled by
The life you give

Laid real low,
For a shorter time,
Dulled back then,
But now you shine,
You suffered then,
You drank the cup
But now you're high
And lifted up,

And here it is
For all to see
The glory of
Your majesty,
The empty cross
There in the ground
The signpost for
The lost and found,

22.   The Streets of Jerusalem

Hosannas now,
Crucify then,
The crowd will chant,
In streets when,
The King proceeds,
In front of them,
On the streets,
Of Jerusalem.

 And Palms will fall,
Like tears soon will,
And wills will break,
And blood will spill,
And the face will fall,
That made all of them,
Down in the dust, of the streets,
Of Jerusalem.

Lauded now,
But bloodied then,
Amidst the cheers,
And jeers of men,
The donkey now,
Will carry him,
But he will carry,
The cross and them,
And drag the heavy weight of sin,
Out through the streets, of Jerusalem,
And make a spectacle of sin,
On the streets,
Of Jerusalem.

Hosanna to The King on high,
Hosanna to the heir of David's line,
He's come to rule,
He's come to die,
He's come to lay down,
His life for them,
Down on the streets,
Of Jerusalem.

23.   Modern Woes

I tell you woe to people like these,

They won't shake your hand

In case they catch some disease,

Yet wherever they go

They continually sneeze,

They'll give you discomfort,

So they feel at ease,

They delouse your cat,

Yet they're covered in fleas,

I tell you woe to people like these.

I tell you woe to people like these,

They won't help you out,

Because they're on their knees,

Praying for you,

While you swing in the breeze,

Give you a dustpan,

While you stand in debris

From your recently imploded life,

They say "please...

I think you missed a bit..."

I tell you woe to people like these,

I tell you woe to people like this,

Nice to your face,

But to your back, it's a diss,

Their loving words are as kind,

As Judas' last Kiss,

I tell you woe to people like this.

I tell you woe to people like this.

They think they're all that,

But they're less hit, more miss,

Living the life-style,

Blowing the kiss,

Looking down on the poor

While in debt to the rich,

I tell you woe to people like this,

They've had they're reward,

All they clenched in their fist,

A hand full of fairy dust,

That disappears like the mist,

In the first light of day, like loves' latest tryst,

The bed is all empty,

You won't be missed,

I tell you woe to people like this.

I tell you woe to people like those,

Who cried 'help the homeless,

Lets give them warm clothes',

But when crossing them, huddled,

In the door of Waitrose,

Last December, they rather conveniently

Froze,

Inactive and glued to the spot,

By their toes,

I tell you woe, to people like those,

I tell you woe to people like you,

Who think that you're clean,

In all that you do,

Outside; all porcelain,

Inside; all Loo,

Making a show,

If only they knew,

You think you've arrived,

When really you're through,

Your body is old,

But your facelift is new,

You're fooling no-one, least of all you,

Woe to people like you

Woe to the whitewashed tombs,

Woe to the face of it,

Woe to perfume,

That covers the scent,

Which comes from the gloom,

The rotting of bones,

Stored in your room,

The skeleton closet,

Closest to discovery soon,

Woe to white house and woe to the room,

Woe to the white picket fence,

Woe to the chintz,

And to the pretence,

Woe to the death that it marks,

Death by degrees, died in the dark

While outside is all sweetness and light,

The tomb dressed for Sunday,

In the brightest of white,

Time to get clean from within,

Break open the tomb,

Dig up the sin,

Pour it all out on display,

And pray for the waters to wash it away.

24.   Blip

These feelings
These thoughts

A Blip

This regret
Those oughts'

A Blip

This acceptance
That rejection

A Blip

This loss
This projection

A Blip

This separation
This Isolation

A Blip

This wilderness
This desolation

A Blip

This Pain
This undoing

A Blip

This brick wall
And the ensuing

A Blip

This Long dark night
This sorrows' endurance

A Blip

This wait till the Joy of morning
This wait for reassurance

A Blip

These light and momentary troubles
These years on eternity's line of time

A Blip

A blip in time, in the light
Of the eternal weight of Glory's shine

A Blip.

Hold on.

Just a blip.

25.   Little Deaths

The wise man told me,
That every day,
Is full of little deaths;
Dying wishes.
Dying breaths.

That if in each tiny,
Microcosmic dying,
We meet our maker,
Within the sighing,

Then we can start
Our dying well,
That in the end,
Our life will tell,

That the sting has met its salve,
That fear shall no longer imprison,
Our hearts resolve,

In the letting go,
We go home,
In the lifeless husk,
A seed is sown,

In dying a little,
Every dying day,
In losing all,
We find our way,

When life is full,
Of dying well,
Then heaven holds,
No fear of hell,

So give me this day,
My daily death,
Give me my bread,
As you give me breath,

Give me my life,
As you give me my cross,
To live and die for you,
And not count the loss.

26.   Before

Before the foundation
was laid, The lamb,
Was slain, proclaimed,
The great I am,

Before Moses, before Abraham,
Before Adam gave a damn,

Before the problem,
The solution was formed,
Before the first skin,
Was ever warmed,
Before the Sun,
Was the custodian,
Of all that is old,
The new thing is done,
Before it unfolds,

In the Heart of God,
It's finished, it is done,
The ancient eyes,
On what's to become,
Late in time,
Behold him, Son,
Before the battle,
The fight is won,

And as Adam walked,
In new felt shame,
The word, was as naked,
As candle flame,
The light was the life of men,
And we behold his glory,
Now as then,

He shone in the darkness,
Not that darkness could understand,
To give light to the whole house,
He put him on a stand,

In the beginning.

27.   Flint-Face

Set my face like flint,
Face into the sun,
Don't squint,
Turn towards the wind,
Don't blink,
Slitted eyes, fixed prize,
Don't teeter on the brink,

Face into the sun,
Not bursts, don't run
Just walk till you can't
Walk then some more,
Tired calloused feet
Stone hardened floor,
Set your face,
Like cooling Iron,
Molten no more,
Set for Zion,

Flinted sharp,
Like the prow of a ship,
Raised chin, stout lip,
Firm grip, on walking stick,
The belt and sword,
Swinging round my hip,
Don't fall
Can't slip
Flint faced for the finished race,

Come desert Sun,
Come Hurricane,
Come avalanche,
Come Monsoon rain,

I'm flint-faced,
For the finished race,

I'm steely eyed,
For the final prize,

I've set my face,
To see grace,
In the expression of,
My saviours face.

28.   Wordless

It is here

In my wordless prayer

I still my soul

To meet you there

My words betray

My anxious thought

And so I kneel before you

As I ought

My inner longings

Long have taught

That my outward strivings

Will come to naught

So wordless I

Let my heart be caught

Adopt the posture

Let hands be raised

Let life be rendered

In ceaseless praise

Let all I am,

Without a noise,

Lift my life

As my loving voice

That all my deeds

Proclaim your love

Hearts and hands

And head above

Lost in praise

And wordless love

29.   Skullduggery

Golgotha,

The place of the skull,

where the lamb and the scapegoat

Were dragged for the cull,

Splayed and stretched out ,

Side by side,

 Innocence,

Guilt and pride,

Matryoshka,

In The Inside,

They crucified a lamb,

But a Lion would rise,

You thought this was a criminal,

Convicted and tried,

You thought this was a saviour,

But save your eyes,

The greatest heist,

Job done from the inside,

Stole back life,

To give to his bride,

The hero died,

But he also survived

And those driving the death,

Were merely along for the ride

In all of their pride and their thuggery,

This plain-hiding scheme could have seemed,

Like Skulduggery,

It was 'probably a robbery'

Eloi, Eloi,

Lama sabachthani

You forsook, what it took,

But now you've come back to me,

Hosanna

Maranatha,

Hallelujah,

Golgotha,

30.   Doorkeep

Rather than a selfish life,
Filled with every luxury,
Preferable to poverty and porcine envy,
I said I'd be a doorkeeper,
A hired servant.
If the remains of my life were to last only a day, in your
presence,
It would outweigh all the wanting,
Of a thousand filled with every indulgence,

But

I have to be honest boss,
I have to be straight with you, Dad,
I'd take that,
I would.

I'd take it and be grateful,
It's more than I deserve or could ever ask for,
But I' can't help but hope for something more,

It's not the robes or the ring,
It's not the fatted calf, or any other thing,
It's the bit where you fall on me,
And welcome me in,
To your house,

Forever,

It's the bit where I get to spend forever as your son,
Daddy, I'll take the Doorkeep's job.
I'd bite your arm of for it,
But, forgive me,

I want so much more.

Christ Jesus came into the world to save sinners—of whom I am the worst.

~1 Timothy 1:15~

31.   Not in The Thunder

For all your light shows

And all the right showings

For your crowds of baying, praising enthusiasts

For your stadium shaking thunderous bass

And ethereal wailings

Your many harmonies

And the thudding of the drums

Mirroring heartbeat syncopations

And a noise that would wake nations

From their slumber

There is the figure of one

within your number

Who stands with arms folded

He wasn't in the Thunder

Nor the earthquake

Nor was he any less in them

Whatever turf you take

There is a man,

In a bedroom somewhere

Who realises for the first time

That The Son of God himself

Knew what it was

To fear God

For all the thunder

And what goes on under

For absence of the quake

His shoulders start to shake

Even to know him in perfect love

Is still to fear him.

Even the most intimate son

Revered him.

And this is the love

He has bestowed.

Now, make some noise.

32.   Gong

The symbolism is all wrong,
Whilst the noise of activity goes on and on,
And in the heavenlies, there's a clanging gong,
Summons you, to a tuneless, loveless song,
And to it the misdirected masses flock and throng,

To get a look at what's going on,
This clashing cymbal,
This clanging gong,

How long, how long,
How long has this been going on,

If I surrender all I have to the flames,
If I do it all, in Jesus' name,
But have not love, then to my shame,
I'm reduced to dust,
For the lust of Cain,
And pity me that I ever came,
For the beginning and the end's the same,
Your bristles rose when the clatter came,
So, sound the gong for the latter rain,

And yes, we can all prophesy,
Interpret every groan and sigh,
And dream as the whole world passes by,
But without love, we live a lie,
And life is a death that we're doomed to die,

A death cry that we're doomed to hear,
The cracking sound of our dry veneer,
The hollow noise: your only Souvenir,
Of all you have achieved down here,
So, take it in, blow it out your rear,
We'll all be out upon our ear,
On a ghost ship with no one to steer,
Without the love,
We'll drown in fear,

I speak in tongues,
But still you hear,
I said:
Without love,
We drown in fear,

Without love a worthless all,
A blind stumbling down an endless hallway,
Extended hands to prevent a fall,
They feel your way down a ceaseless wall,
Your voice is a husk from your all your dry calls,

Your calls that have gone on so long,
Like a clashing cymbal,
A clanging gong,
The symbolism is all wrong,

You gain the world,
You beat the gong,

You gain the world,
You beat the gong.

33.   We Sang

We sang 'Holy Spirit come',
And then we went home,
Did he turn up later on,
Alone in that room?

Did he brood over the face,
Of the kick drum and snares?
Did he pour out his love
Over our empty chairs?

Did his still presence
Descend on the keys?
Did the microphone stand,
In still silence and peace?

Did the power point suddenly
Splutter into life,
To point out that power
Can exist in the strife?

Did he linger then,
Eliciting praise,
But no voices nor heads,
Nor hands could be raised,
Because we'd departed,
And gone on our ways?

Come Jesus, we said,
Come Spirit we'd state,
And turn on our heels,
And make for the gate,

If the Spirit will,
Why then won't we wait?

34.   Extremities

Hands held by nails,
Feet impaled,
You always go to extremities,
To show us your love,

Hands healed,
Feet heeled,
You walked a thousand miles,
To show us your love,

Feet held,
While hands washed,
You took the towel.
Before the power,
You always go to such extremities,
To show us your love,

Feet Scarred,
Hands holed,
Forever you will bear the mark,
Of the extremities you will go to,
To show us your love.

35. Pleasant Disciplines & Painless Lessons

Look at me
Looking for
Those easy fixes
And short cuts to holiness
"Where", I ask, "are those pleasant disciplines"
"Where is the painless lesson?"

When your word forewarns us all.
No discipline is pleasant,
But painful.
However,
If learned from,
Produces a harvest of righteousness,
At the right time.

And in your discipline,
Though I can't see it through my tears,
You are showing me,
Your precious and costly love.

36. Truth-Holder

When all about you lose their way

And your voice is lost in all the fray,

When your argument holds no sway,

Hold on to the truth and say,

I hold to the truth in all I do,

But remember it's the truth that's holding you,

When the truth is all the battle ground

When lines are blurred, and scarcely found

And when they're found they're rarely sound,

Know that trends go round and round,

But truth's eternal, through and through

Though you hold the truth,

In truth,

The truth is holding you,

Hold on to truth as best you can

When nothing seems to go to plan

And though you question, know this man,

The truth is Jesus said 'I am'

The truth, the way and life too,

And though you hold to truth,

The truth is, The truth is holding you,

37. Fourteen One

The Fatherless Children of Chance

Born of good luck and happenstance

Alone in the wide universe

Alone and alive without blessing or curse

To do and be done as they might

Without a reason or wrong or a right

And reason's alright as it goes

And for all that I do, I've got one of those

But there's no reason for reason at all

It's dog eating dog or the last one to fall

In the end were all the dust that we came from

And meanings mean nothing without explanation

And there's no judge who can cast judgement on me

I proclaim him a myth and I find him unworthy

Go give account to the sand

Go return your body back to the land

You can take this down as verbatim

There's no God, but Oh, do I hate him.

38. A Wobble in My Walk

There's a wobble in my walk
A stumble in my stride
A shyness in my speech
And a humble in my pride

There's a feeling in my thought
A flying in my fall
A stooping as I climb
The loss of gaining all

There's a dying in my life
A living in my death
There's a taking and a taking hold
In letting go and taking my last breath

39. An Honest Poem

I love you all, with sincere love

But I'd leave in a heartbeat

For the promise of heaven

To be pain free

And without ego

I'm a little torn

But that is what my longings say

I never understood before

When Paul says it is better to be with the lord

But I guess I just ran out of hope

Despite transcendent moments

Of this life ever satisfying me

Or of peace that settles like snow

Or true silence

I love this world but I'm ready to go when the time comes

I love everyone

No, really

Don't think I don't hate objectionable things

But I never met a human who didn't have something to love in them

How ever hard they tried

To convince me otherwise,

And if I was spikey

or hurtful

Or insensitive

Please accept

It was never hate

But fear that kept me from loving you well

And I feel

That the fog of hatred over humanity

would be burned up

if we all could see clearly

The source of our fear

God is love

That is my discovery

But I recommend you don't make the mistake

Of making a God of what or who you love

Submission to a loving and wise God is the furthest thing from subjugation

On the contrary: it is empowerment, if you could only accept his rule

I believe you reject it at your peril

I believe there is one way out

One Human who can save you

The Human Jesus Christ

The bridge across the chasm

of misunderstanding and foolish action

That so many of you automatically rule him out seems like an evidence to me that he is for real

I found him

And was found by him at the age of 6

Yes 6

And I knew something was different

And it never left me

However hard I tried to make it

Because I believe love to be eternal

I'm sorry for all the bad I have done

And to the people I have hurt

Nothing I gained from hurting you was worth it

Please forgive me

Though I can't always show it

And the truth of these words may not be known

Till the end of what is known to us now

I love you

And if you hurt me

I forgive you

Every last one of you

40. In Every Place

In every place

He is

He took me to a high place,

And showed me,

Over the contours of my kingdom,

My corner of the county,

The small stretch of a score of miles,

In which I live out the majority of my life,

In the basin,

And over the valley,

Where the wind whistles,

On the peaks,

And above,

Amidst clouds,

In clear skies,

Behind the wing,

Above the bird's back

All about it

And far, far off,

And every space in-between,

The camera is rolling,

And always was,

Our lives go on beneath him,

Within him,

And he within,

Cars and busses, busy on their way,

As they pass through he is with them,

And he remains with them,

Until they reach their destination,

Even if it is The other side of the country,

And yet he never leaves this place,

The camera is still rolling here,

And when tomorrow morning,

I rise early with the thought of this poem,

He is still here,

In the darkness,

As the larks wake,

And there he is too with the poet,

In his head,

And surrounding his half-clad body,

And in the space between his fingers,

And the keys,

As they repeatedly drum on the squares,

That send the signals,

That tell his computer to display the letters they encase,

Upon his screen,

The ones you are reading right now,

And not only is he there between the poets fingers and letters,

But he is with you,

And he is still here,

Hovering over the valley,

Filling the space

Between hills and blood cells alike,

And in every lonely place

In every corner and nook,

On mountain tops,

In desert,

Across vast tundra,

Over waters,

Beneath the ice,

In every space an eye could see,

And in the eye itself

The camera never stops rolling,

He is

Existing

Wild and free,

And we

Have only just arrived

In his eternity.

"You shall know the truth, and the truth shall set you free"

~Jesus Christ, John 8:32~

Printed in Great Britain
by Amazon

26732169R00045